M000304710

midnight meditations *for* moms

calming comfort
FOR THE
wee hours

miranda hersey

CASTLE POINT BOOKS
NEW YORK

www.castlepointbooks.com

The Castle Point Books trademark is owned by
Castle Point Publishing, LLC. Castle Point books are
published and distributed by St. Martin's Publishing Group.

ISBN 978-1-250-27536-3 (paper over board)
ISBN 978-1-250-27537-0 (ebook)

Images used under license from Shutterstock.com

Our books may be purchased in bulk for
promotional, educational, or business use.

Please contact your local bookseller or the Macmillan Corporate
and Premium Sales Department at 1-800-221-7945, extension 5442,
or by email at MacmillanSpecialMarkets@macmillan.com.

First Edition: 2021

10 9 8 7 6 5 4 3 2 1

these moments of peace belong to:

_____

contents

* * *

Introduction	6		Planning	34
Perfection	8		Challenges	36
Listening	10		Sisterhood	38
Self-Care	12		Boundaries	40
Stillness	14		Hands	42
Resources	16		Anxiety	44
Dawn	18		Busyness	46
Moonlight	20		Aspirations	48
Timing	22		Weariness	50
Why	24		Pace	52
Happiness	26		Support	54
Body	28		Improvisation	56
Phases	30		Contribution	58
Intuition	32		Questions	60

Responding	62	Windows	112
Moments	64	Labels	114
Release	66	Eyes	116
Awakening	68	Joy	118
Shifts	70	Truth	120
Shoulds	72	Rhythm	122
Oasis	74	Meditation	124
Advocate	76	Sadness	126
Reconnection	78	Creed	128
Adolescence	80	Home	130
Emotions	82	Goals	132
Childhood	84	Creativity	134
Focus	86	Basics	136
Regret	88	Grown	138
Authenticity	90	Occasions	140
Community	92	Seasons	142
Sick Days	94	Learning	144
Inheritance	96	Thoughts	146
Appreciation	98	Laughter	148
Individuality	100	Restoration	150
Honesty	102	Comparison	152
Nature	104	Movement	154
Presence	106	Shield	156
Self-Healing	108	Journey	158
Growing	110		

introduction

It's easy to romanticize midnight motherhood as the tender and dimly lit rocking, feeding, and changing of a tiny baby. But we quickly discover the wee hours hold so much more that calls us from sleep at all ages and stages: sickness, distress, the bad dream, the sleepover gone awry, the curfew-tester. Sometimes it's our own natural worries, fears, and emotions that keep us awake. In the nighttime hours when the house is quiet, our minds may be anything but still.

Whatever has stirred you from sleep, know that you are not alone. You are embraced in the circle of motherhood as we navigate this journey together and

find support for the physical, emotional, and mental stamina that motherhood asks of us. Consider this book your night shift companion, soothing the weary mama with gentle centering, reconnection, and reflection. Each meditation seeks to settle your mind, body, and heart. Read these pages in any way you find most comforting: one page a night or many; sequentially, by topic, or at random.

Motherhood doesn't come with flexible hours, but we can find moments of peace within the night shifts. May the pages of *Midnight Meditations for Moms* hold that space for you.

tonight,
*I let go of
perfection.*

I embrace myself as a mother in all my perceived shortcomings and flaws.

* * *

No one is as hard on me as I am. Instinctively, I want to raise my child with the positive experiences and comforts of my own childhood—and without what I found painful. I want to be a mother who meets every challenge with grace, who doesn't succumb to frustration. Yet I accept that perfection is not real. Not for me, not for anyone.

*Every day,
I strive to do my best.
And when I don't meet my ideal,
I can give myself the same
empathy and understanding
that I give to my child.
This is love.*

tonight,
I listen.

10

I notice with curiosity that all sounds seem louder at night.

* * *

Sometimes, in the quiet, I hear the refrigerator hum, crickets through an open window, the passing of a late-night car or distant train. In the sweetest moments, I hear the rhythmic breathing of my loved ones as they succumb to sleep. On other nights, restlessness or crying fills my ears and hurts my heart. Even in the dark hours of lingering upset and illness, I know that these sounds, like all sounds, will ultimately ebb into stillness.

I remain present in what I hear, remembering that dawn always breaks, returning us to the sounds of a new day and all its promise.

tonight,
I reflect on caring for my loved ones.

I am steadfast in my commitment to motherhood and all that it encompasses.

* * *

My days are full and my list is long. With so much to do, it is often easier to postpone or ignore taking care of myself. But tending to my own needs—physical, emotional, mental, spiritual—is essential to being the mother and the person I want to be. In order to be there for others, I need to be there for myself.

I am a better, happier person when I make time to do the things that no one else can do for me. Self-care is my responsibility and a life-giving practice I want to model for my child.

13

tonight,
I surrender to the stillness.

I embrace the intimacy of this moment: I am simply tending to my child.

* * *

Time moves more slowly in the dark. I don't have anywhere else to be; I don't have anything else to do. No phone calls or texts, no one waiting to hear from me, no errands, work, or traffic jams. My focus is simply to show love and feel the bond between mother and child. The realm of my experience accordions into the here and now.

I might rather be sleeping, but I can appreciate the gentle respite of this hour and the connection with my child.

tonight,

I marvel at new strength.

I reflect on the tool set that arrived with my child.

* * *

Motherhood has revealed within me an inventory of inner resources I didn't know I had. With no measurable prequalification, I'm able to accomplish the everyday miracle of keeping a young human alive. Each morning I get up and navigate an ever-changing landscape while doing hard things I've never done before. Amazingly, I make this happen even within the constraints of broken sleep.

_I have strengths,
instincts, and aptitudes
I don't always
recognize._

tonight,
I am grateful for new beginnings.

I look to the morning light that softens yesterday's hard edges.

* * *

No matter what happened yesterday, and no matter how I feel about it, every morning I get a fresh start. The dawn reminds me that all things are possible. I can use that new beginning however I want, in ways big or small, or not at all. Amazingly, the day after that, another new beginning will arrive. I reopen this brilliant gift every morning.

*With intention
and curiosity, I turn over
each morning leaf in wonder,
fresh with possibility.*

tonight,

I observe the moonlight.

**I feel connected
within this contrast of
light and dark.**

* * *

When the moon is full and the sky is clear, moonbeams
spill shadows bright as those cast by the sun. Filtering
through windows, moonlight washes cool monochrome
over the familiar shapes and colors of this room. In the
wee hours of motherhood, moonlight is a quiet and
soothing companion, waxing and waning in its monthly
metronome. It has kept company to a lineage of humans
awake in the night over tens of thousands of years.

----

*Observing the moon
connects me to all those
who came before,
gazed up at the night sky,
and wondered.*

----

tonight,
I consider
the timetable
of my life.

**I see that in the bigger picture
of what happens and when,
I am never late or early.**

* * *

I am always right on time—because the stages, events, and milestones of my life happen when they do. I don't always like or understand this mysterious chronology, but I can trust in its ultimate cohesion, even when I'm too close to see it.

_Everything I experience leads me to
an hour in the distant future
when I look back and say yes,
I see all that came to pass
conspired for me to be here right now,
the only place I could ever be._

tonight,
*I remember
the why.*

24

Sometimes, too much of my day is spent doing things I don't want to do but have to do.

* * *

Looking closely, I see that most of my chores or unappealing tasks are directly connected to my core values. My "why" for cleaning the kitchen could be that I feel good when my kitchen is clean—and a home that feels good to its residents is important to me. In unraveling my "have-to" list, I see arrows that connect to what matters.

———————————————

Reminding myself of my overarching values keeps me from becoming overwhelmed and helps me realize that I'm actually doing what I want to do.

———————————————

tonight,

I envision happiness.

**I remember that I,
like all beings, have a
right to happiness.**

* * *

Feeling good, secure, and comfortable isn't a reward for good behavior. I don't need to condone or perpetuate circumstances that are at odds with my emotional well-being. When a situation is complicated or difficult, I might tell myself I expect too much, that I'm being unrealistic, that my standards are too high. But perpetuating conditions that don't feel good only serves to postpone or deny the happiness I deserve.

*I can cultivate joy
and the conditions
that foster my happiness.*

tonight, *I give thanks for my body.*

**I celebrate this
physical form as the conduit
of my human experience.**

* * *

While I don't always provide my body with optimal
care, my body holds no resentment (although it does
sometimes complain). This body, this constant and
truthful companion, has done amazing things for me.
My body engages and channels my physical senses,
enabling me to observe, understand, and interact with
the world in many different ways. My body propels me
to do what needs doing, no matter how tired I am.

_It is my body that
holds and cares for my child—
a wondrous capacity that
I observe with gratitude._

tonight,
I reflect on phases.

I ponder the parenting challenges that come and go.

* * *

Certain occurrences and episodes of infancy, childhood, and adolescence are sometimes minimized by well-meaning loved ones and observers as "just a phase." While the intent of this counsel is "take heart—it won't last forever," a stretch of parenting challenges coupled with sleepless nights can be disorienting. In this laden state of mind, a so-called phase may feel like an unwanted and semi-permanent lifestyle change. But I know it's not.

I remind myself of the truth: Babies don't cry forever, and by the age of eighteen, most kids are toilet-trained, dry overnight, and don't bite their classmates.

tonight,
I honor intuition.

**I listen for the voice inside
that knows what to do,
even when I don't.**

* * *

Sometimes this voice is soft, almost imperceptible, but it's always there. It's a knowing, a gift of information or direction, that registers in my body like it came from somewhere else. Whether this voice is muffled or vibrant, the more I focus on how it sounds and feels, the more clearly I hear it—and the more clearly I hear it, the stronger it gets.

*When I listen with intention
and heed its wise guidance,
my intuition thrives.*

tonight,

I plan for tomorrow.

I envision what my day will look like.

* * *

I take a moment to identify the three most important things I'd like to get done tomorrow, creating a mental or physical list. When my days are difficult or otherwise consumed, a single most important thing will suffice. I estimate how much time I need for this list, and I target a time frame for the doing.

When tomorrow comes,
I can navigate the day with my
map in hand, rerouting as necessary
and steering clear of guilt
for what doesn't get done.

----

tonight,
I think about doing what is difficult.

I have already done many hard things.

* * *

I have learned and expanded in the realization of each challenging circumstance. When I doubt my ability to address something large and consequential, I can let go of the fear. I remember my strengths and I remember my courage. I look at where I am now and all that I have overcome. Doing hard things serves my process of self-discovery.

----

*I already have
the necessary muscles;
I need only to flex and warm up.
I have faith in myself.*

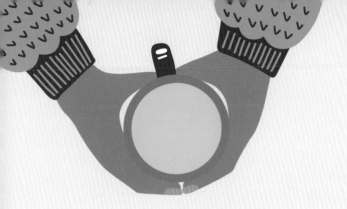

tonight,

I connect with my sisters in motherhood.

I am not alone in the experience of mothering.

*** *** ***

As darkness curls around the earth, at this very moment, millions of other women are also awake and taking care of children in the night. Connected by gossamer threads of familiarity, we can find comfort in this unspoken sisterhood. Many of our paths overlap and intertwine as we encounter trials, wonders, and elations. I know that even in my darkest hours, other mothers are facing similar difficulties. I feel compassion for these sisters, as I do for myself.

_____

*May all of us,
and all of our children,
know peaceful hearts
beneath the night sky.*

_____

tonight,

I promise to stand up for myself.

I clarify boundaries and how I feel about mine.

* * *

It takes practice to recognize when interactions, requests, relationships, or situations don't feel right. It takes even more practice to learn to say no and proactively self-advocate. How do I engage with people who make me feel uncomfortable? Are these relationships unavoidable or unchangeable? On a daily basis, I model for my child how I do and do not allow others to treat me. Am I demonstrating appropriate self-care and self-protection?

Exercising my boundaries shows my child how to practice this essential skill.

tonight,
*I see
my child's
hands.*

**I wonder what
these hands will one day
discover and create.**

* * *

These young hands, which first looked like tiny starfish, will one day be impossibly grown and capable. Will I still recognize the shape of these fingers? I want to memorize my child's hands exactly as they are: whether little shell fingernails or growing nails with the dirt of discovery embedded beneath; the lines that map these palms; the way knuckles curve into a small fist.

---

*Holding a small,
soft hand, I dream of all
that is yet to come
as my child meets the world.*

tonight,
*I observe
anxiety.*

I know where anxiety manifests in my body.

* * *

Fear, dread, and worry are different notes on the same scale, ranging from unconscious fretting to uncomfortable preoccupation to the elevated heart rate and shortened breath of full-blown alarm. Fear thrives in unlit, unopened places, in the unpleasant murk of "what if?" I know that anxiety isn't useful. I relax my body, breathe deeply, and meet this fear: What is the worst that could happen in this situation? What would I do if that happened? And then what? And then what?

When I define its shape and my response, anxiety is just a shadow on the wall.

tonight,
I honor the doing of nothing.

I think about
the busyness of life.

* * *

On some days, I wring the most from every minute.
I am a paragon of awareness and productivity and
accomplishment and checkmarks on my list. I take it
all in and give it all out. On other days, not so much.
I'm resistant. I don't want to do all the things.
Disengagement doesn't mean I'm doing it wrong; it
means I need a break. I can pull back and surrender
to being instead of doing. I can allow myself minimal
output while I recharge.

Now and then,
"wasting" time is the best way
for me to spend it.

tonight,

I see through my child's eyes.

I step back and wonder how my child perceives me as a mother.

* * *

Reflecting on the present moment and envisioning our distant future, how would I like my child to one day look back and describe me? I think of the mothers I admire, and why. Of the many possibilities, which words best capture my aspirations of motherhood? Are these ideals authentic to who I am? What feels right and true?

Thinking of how
I'd like my child to see me today
and in years to come,
I reconnect to what I value most
in mothering.

tonight,

*I am
tired.*

I feel fatigue as a force that washes through me, over me.

* * *

In motherhood, I have felt a depth of exhaustion beyond what I thought possible. When I am this tired, I have no room for anything else. I will do what needs doing as I am able, and that will be enough. One day, a viable sleep schedule will return, and this cloud of weariness will lift.

The late nights of motherhood do not last forever—and one day I may well look back on these midnight moments with fondness and nostalgia.

tonight, *I contemplate the passage of time.*

**Some days are short,
some are long, and
others feel endless.**

* * *

But each year seems to accelerate and pass more quickly than the one before. Weeks and months fly by at warp speed. Entire days seem to vanish when I turn around. Wanting to savor the sweetest parts of my child's life and development, I acknowledge the variable speed of this clock and calendar.

*To slow my pace
and imprint these memories,
I can practice showing up with
intention, curiosity,
and all of my senses.*

I value the supportive people in my life.

* * *

As a mother, giving is a daily practice, but receiving is less familiar and often feels less natural. Just when a helping hand could make a difference, sometimes it feels easier to launch into solitary orbit and do it all myself. I keep in mind the relationships based on family or friendship that are real and secure. It feels good to remember that when I need help, I can ask the people who care about me for what I need.

_____ _____ ____

*Just as I want to support
the people I care about,
they too want to help me
as they are able.*

_____ _____ ____

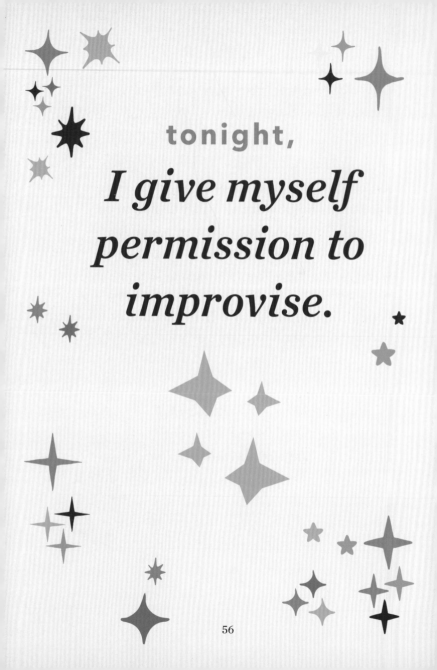

tonight,
*I give myself
permission to
improvise.*

**No matter how much I plan
and prepare, motherhood teems
with the unexpected.**

* * *

At any given moment I may need to change or abandon my
present focus or activity because I need to do something
else. Even when I'm not in the mood to be flexible, I know
how to recalculate and adjust. With this perspective, I can
look back and admire my ability to ad-lib, invent, problem
solve, redirect, and sidestep, making decisions with the
instincts and information at hand.

*It's okay to make it up as I go along.
Sometimes, my adaptability and
spontaneity lead to pleasant surprises.*

tonight,

I consider responsibility.

I imagine teaching responsibility to my child.

* * *

It's important for my child to feel like a capable and contributing member of our family and our community. Even when it's easier to just do it myself, encouraging my child to be engaged, responsible, and accountable serves us both better now and in the long run. Practicing responsibility builds self-esteem and identity, guiding my child along the path toward self-actualized and self-sufficient adulthood.

—————————————— ——— ——

As my child gradually
takes on responsibilities over time,
the more helpful those
contributions become,
which is positive for both of us.

—————————————— ——— ——

tonight,
*I accept
uncertainty.*

**I admit that I can't know
what tomorrow brings.**

* * *

I acknowledge the cloud of question marks gathered
on the horizon at any given moment, some hovering
faintly, others flashing in neon. I can't know what the
future holds for me, or for my child. The more I am able
to embrace the mystery of this human experience, the
more at ease I become. While I can't control what
happens before it gets here, I can and will respond
when it does.

----

*I always manage to do
what needs doing.
I always have. I can practice
getting comfortable
with not knowing.*

tonight,
I choose my response.

I reflect on
reaction versus response
in addressing conflict.

* * *

When experiencing disappointment, hurt, or anger, reacting impulsively may exacerbate the issue. Instead, I can respond with intention and integrity. The choice is always mine. By determining my priority in any interaction, and filtering my impulses through those objectives, I am better able to respond with what the moment requires. What outcome best serves my bigger picture? By responding rather than reacting, I model self-regulation for my child.

*When I respond
rather than react,
I am more connected
to what matters.*

tonight,
I consider impermanence.

I know that the present moment will subside.

* * *

Whether I label an experience positive or I label it negative, the only surety is that it will pass. Letting the most joyful moments go is sometimes bittersweet. But clinging to the present is to clutch at water with fists. By accepting the truth of transience, I can hold the lovely minutes lightly, allow the difficult moments to recede, and fill up on what is.

Gifts of experience
come to me with each new day,
continuous as sunrise.

----

tonight,
I relax my body.

**I invite the comfort of
a gentle unwinding.**

* * *

Starting with my face, slowly and intentionally, I soften my forehead and jaw; moving down to my neck and shoulders, I search for areas of tightness and contraction. I take several long, deep breaths, in and out, fully expanding my lungs. Descending slowly to my abdomen, I allow tension to release; down through my hips and legs all the way to my toes, I relax my body, loosening each muscle, lingering in the tight places as needed, pausing and breathing in relaxation.

_____

*At any time of day or night,
this practice can bring me back
into my body, making me more at ease
and centered in the now.*

_____

tonight,
I invite the morning.

I envision how I'd like to wake up tomorrow.

* * *

After I sleep—for however long I'm able—the day will begin. I envision those first few hours unfurling. I accept the variables I can control, and I acknowledge those that I can't. Whether I have a full schedule or a blank page, I set intentions for how I'd like the morning to be. I can think of at least one thing to look forward to, no matter how small.

———————————————

Carrying this vision loosely,
I can awaken to the new day
with an easy heart and embrace
what the morning brings.

———————————————

tonight,

*I see
the shifts.*

**I look at how motherhood changes
the way I conceive of myself.**

* * *

The twists and turns of this extraordinary journey
shape me in ways I could not have imagined or prepared
for. My sphere of being has both expanded and
contracted. Envisioning myself then and now, I see
where my feelings, perspectives, and identity have
changed—and where they have not. With intention and
inquiry, the experience of motherhood can deepen my
sense of self and connection to priorities.

*This remarkable path
continually provides opportunities
to know myself—
and I will welcome them.*

tonight,

I free myself from "should."

**I look for ways to
lighten the internal pressure
that weighs me down.**

* * *

Shoulds are things I don't really want to do—and don't
really have to do, either. They're the things that sit
uncomfortably in the middle, waiting to become action
items while periodically poking me with procrastination
guilt. I can check my shoulds to see whether any are
actually wants or have-tos. Then I can filter the
remaining shoulds for things I can delegate or delete.

_____

*While I may never reach
should-zero, I can reduce the ways
in which I pressure myself
to do things that I don't want
or have to do.*

_____

tonight,

I conjure my private oasis.

I envision a place, real or imaginary,
in which I feel wonderful.

* * *

I envision an environment that empowers me to be myself without criticism, concession, or shame. Picturing this place in vivid detail, I consider: How does it look, sound, and smell? What does this space feel like? What are its comforts? Breathing deeply, I relax, recenter, and reconnect. Nothing here needs doing. I am able to soften and hear my intuition.

*Whenever I'm at loose ends
in the present moment,
this private and restorative world
is only ever a thought away.*

tonight,
I think about advocating for my child.

I remember that nobody knows my child as I do.

* * *

In many contexts, I serve as my child's voice and primary advocate. And in certain subtle ways, I am uniquely able to see and hear and understand my child. When I can tell something is amiss—physical, mental, or emotional—I feel the resulting discomfort in my core. It's a visceral and protective response that prompts action when needed. It's a gift of motherhood.

*I am able to advocate
for my child with a strength
fueled by knowing what
no one else can know.*

tonight,

*I remember
who I
wanted to be.*

**I think of all the best selves
I have envisioned over time.**

* * *

I contemplate all the divergent paths I once wanted
to pursue; the lives I wanted to inhabit; the person
I aspired to become. Among all the shimmering
filaments I've let go, some fell away naturally and
others slipped through my open hands, sometimes
while I wasn't looking. Remembering all that once held
promise, I comb for strands that still glimmer. Is it
time to reconnect with hopes deferred?

---

*Becoming who I truly want to be is
my profound responsibility and privilege—
and lights a path for my child to discover
authentic joy as well.*

tonight,
I flash back to adolescence.

I remember my own metamorphosis into and experience as a teenager.

* * *

I recollect what I wanted and what I was afraid of; who I loved and by whom I felt loved. I reach back to how I felt about my independence, my sense of agency, and the adults who understood me and those who didn't. Today, in preparing my child for adulthood and self-sufficiency, I can meet increased maturity and responsibility with greater freedom and autonomy.

The more I stay in touch with the adolescent of my past, the less conflict I'll have with the adolescent of my present or future.

tonight,

I tune in to how I feel.

I think about how emotions manifest.

* * *

Where in my body do I experience specific emotions? Which feelings lodge in my throat, chest, shoulders, stomach, bones, heart, or behind my eyes? Some emotions are difficult to locate or identify, particularly when several different feelings coincide. When discomfort arises, it's tempting to squelch what I'm feeling or look the other way. Staying with how I feel may be uncomfortable, but a gentle practice of curiosity encourages my well-being.

The more I know about how I feel,
the more I know about who I am.
In turn, the better equipped I am
as a human and a mother.

tonight,

I see myself
as a child.

I remember that I was once exactly the age that my child is now.

* * *

I think about the environment and circumstances of my life at that time as I understood them to be. Knowing what I know today, as an adult and a mother, I reflect on my small self with empathy, admiration, and tenderness. I think about the differences between my experience and the experience my child is having at this reflection point. Participating in childhood now as a mother, I have new understanding of my own childhood, and I also have new questions.

My perspective on childhood will continue to evolve as my child, and I, grow older. But I can always remind myself to look through a child's eyes.

---

tonight,

I ponder what matters most.

I think about my sphere of investment.

* * *

Knowing that I cannot do all the things all the time, I continually reallocate where and how I focus my attention. Given that hours are nonrenewable and energy is finite, I ask: Is this investment of my mental, emotional, spiritual, and physical self in alignment with my priorities? Is this a circumstance, activity, or relationship in which I want to invest my essential resources? If the answer is no, I can mindfully redirect those assets into closer alignment with my main concerns.

*When I avoid overextending myself
with less important things,
I have more strength and joy
for what matters most.*

tonight,
I step past
regret.

**I contemplate the choices
I made that didn't work out
as I'd hoped.**

* * *

If I could go back and do things differently, perhaps
I would, and perhaps I wouldn't. Everything I have
experienced, everything that has ever happened to me,
has led me to this moment: up at this hour, sitting here,
in this place, the mother of this child. Mistakes and
failures aren't really possible, because this experiential
journey informs my present and shapes my future.
Regret has no purpose in the journey of self-discovery.

*Everything that happens
teaches me something I didn't know
I didn't know.*

I reflect on being seen for who I am.

I celebrate the people
who truly see me.

* * *

Among my family members and friends, I know with whom I feel seen—and with whom I do not. Being seen and accepted affirms my authenticity, and it feels good. In these safe relationships, I can practice being myself. To help my child feel acknowledged in this way, I can release my preconceptions and see my child without judgment. Instead of projecting what's in my head, I can recognize and embrace who my child really is.

———————————————————

For my child and for myself,
learning to be authentic
is more life-giving than
learning to meet expectations.

 ———————————————————

tonight,
I seek connection.

**I picture the communities
I belong to, in all the ways that
I define community.**

* * *

Am I connected to my people as much as I want to be?
Am I finding new people? While motherhood can be
isolating, it comes with membership in an exclusive club.
Some of us gain easy access to this club; others invest
quantities of heartache, time, and money to get here.
In whichever way we earn our maternal credentials,
mothers share a tacit bond: the camaraderie of common
experience. We recognize each other. This community is
one among many where I can find kinship.

*If I am ever in need
of community,
I can foster the connections
that surround me.*

tonight,
I take it easy.

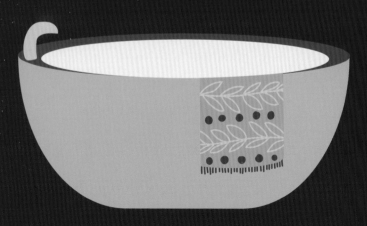

I acknowledge that sick days call for simple standards.

* * *

Motherhood doesn't come with time off. Yet it's hard to take care of other people when I'm sick—even more so when someone I'm taking care of is also under the weather. To navigate illness, I can ask for and accept as much help as I can get. Only the barest essentials matter: food, water, laundry, and medical care.

----

*I can treat myself
with extra gentleness
when illness enters my home,
especially when I don't have
backup or relief.*

tonight,

I honor heritage.

I reflect on my child's intangible inheritance.

* * *

I bring to mind the untold generations of ancestors that stretch back through centuries of connected strangers. I envision the wealth of lives lived and loved and stitched into the fabric of my child's inheritance, the heirlooms that pass through me in real and intuited DNA, through nature and through nurture. I am a product of generational experience, and so is my child.

_____

*As my child and I
navigate our heritage,
we augment this legacy for
generations yet to come.*

- - - - - - - - - - - - - -

tonight,
I take positive stock.

I run through a mental list of what's working well in my life.

* * *

Through a lens of appreciative inquiry, I think about the ways in which I'm thriving. I recollect the elements of my life that bring me joy, the knots I've unraveled, the people and circumstances I feel good about, the things that feel easy, the relationships centered in love. With gratitude and open-mindedness, I step back and affirm good fortune where it blooms. I ask myself: Can I do more of what works? Can I use what works to improve what isn't yet as I'd like it to be?

Looking at my positive inventory, I see much to feel good about and opportunity for more blessings to come.

tonight,
I wonder at
individuality.

I bear in mind how every child, including those raised in the same environment, can have vastly different needs.

* * *

In addition to being unique, each child's needs change over time. This means that previous experience with other children may or may not be relevant to raising this one. Sometimes, nothing I thought I knew seems to apply. I find myself continuously reassessing to gauge for changes in sensitivity, independence, affection, socialization, stimulation, and other needs and preferences—because what worked today might not work tomorrow.

Learning to see what my child needs, and puzzling out how to meet those needs, is the ongoing practice of motherhood.

tonight,

I'm being honest.

I acknowledge that motherhood is not always enjoyable.

* * *

Mothering is a journey of extreme highs and lows, some of which are unpleasant, some of which are challenging, and some of which seem impossible. Some days feel like a domino cascade of things gone wrong. But I can make space for the complicated feelings.

I can feel resentful and annoyed and angry and disappointed without shaming myself for internal honesty. Motherhood is a journey, and there will be bumps in the road.

tonight,
*I turn to
Mother Nature.*

I think about the natural world and its place in my life.

* * *

I recollect the time I spent outdoors in my youth, and the time I spend outdoors as an adult. How does being outside stimulate my senses and my sense of self? How do my lungs and body feel as I breathe deeply in the outdoor air? Whether my experiences involve a forest, an ocean shore, a mountain, a wooded lakeside, or someplace close to home, I recall the mind-and-body impact of my outdoor encounters.

My relationship with the natural world is worth nurturing and sharing with my child, by example and by inclusion.

tonight,
*I value
presence.*

My experiences come alive when I am present and aware.

* * *

I know that presence is living the moment through my senses, not through a digital screen or a veil of preoccupation. Presence is showing up for whatever is happening, even the mundane every day—*especially* the mundane every day. I realize that experience imprints when I slow to the speed of sensation and observation.

I will practice staying with what takes place in front of me, as it emerges, instead of unconsciously dwelling in variables of the future or reruns of the past.

tonight,
I embrace self-healing.

I consider the recuperative power of mothering.

* * *

Looking back on my childhood from a mother's perspective, I contemplate and acknowledge what was missing. As I walk the path of motherhood, I can look for opportunities to creatively give myself what my mother was unable to give. With gentleness, I can care for myself as I wish I'd been cared for years ago. I can advocate for myself, tend to my needs, and ensure my safety and security.

The practice of healing through self-love supports me in mothering my child from the wise perspective of my past.

tonight,

I think about growing pains.

I consider the metamorphic process of growth and what it feels like.

* * *

I'm familiar with the awkward, mysterious ache that sometimes comes with physical and emotional growth. This discomfort is the contraction that precedes expansion into something new. It's a strange and irregular tenderness that often doesn't make sense until the development or evolution becomes identifiable. I perceive this process in my child—sometimes after the fact—and sometimes in myself.

*When I'm out of sorts
or bewildered by puzzle pieces
that don't fit together, I can remember
that the picture will materialize
at the moment of expansion,
in its own time.*

tonight,
*I open windows
of time.*

I can see the minutes around the edges.

* * *

The bits and pieces and scraps of a day can add up to something useful. Where motherhood isn't conducive to long periods of focused work or creativity, minutes add up at the margins of my day. By micro-sizing the tasks of a specific project, I can make an inch or two of progress when a few unclaimed minutes present themselves.

—————————————————

I can use little gifts of time to my advantage, whether for productivity and progress, or for intentionally doing nothing at all.

—————————————————

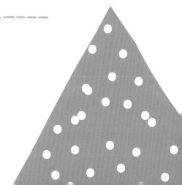

tonight,
I resist the labels.

I illuminate my perceptions of positive and negative.

* * *

Labeling what happens as "good" or "bad" can be reflexive. But labels and their definitions are limiting and prevent me from experiencing what really is. Just as people are not all good or all bad but multifaceted, so too is what occurs. I can observe and allow without the internal metrics of quality and quantity.

—————————————————————

I can practice seeing and being instead of knowing to stay open to the possibility of the moment.

—————————————————————

tonight,

I connect without words.

I reflect on how it feels to look into my child's eyes.

* * *

Eye contact is a wordless connection between two humans, first kindled in the alchemy of early gazes. So much is said and shared in this universal language. As my child grows, we can both engage fully during conversation without the hindrance of digital screens and distractions. I can model eye contact as a practice that says to my child: You matter. This conversation matters and I am listening with all my attention, whatever you want to tell me.

When I make eye contact with my child, I convey presence, interest, and receptivity.

tonight,
I focus on my own joy.

I contemplate how I like to spend my time.

* * *

I take an inner tour of what attracts me, interests me, delights me. What makes me lose myself and find myself all at once? I ponder the ways in which those things have changed over the years—and have continued to evolve in motherhood. I ask: What would I do with my days if livelihood weren't a consideration? Can I find ways to do more of that, in some form, in the present?

Doing what I love
is not a someday project.

tonight,

I embrace my truth.

I examine how I feel, physically and emotionally, when I am authentically myself.

* * *

My body feels a certain way when I do something I don't want to do. Even if I'm unaware, my body knows when I origami my feelings into the shape of someone else's expectations. My physical self registers the denial. Conversely, when I speak and act in keeping with my values, wants, beliefs, needs, and emotions, my body and heart resonate with the honesty.

I can practice respecting my truth and perceiving how the affirmation feels.

tonight,
I reach for
rhythm.

I explore my habits, routines, and schedule.

* * *

Some of my routines are ingrained and don't require much thought. These reliable habits are the structure of my hours, days, and weeks. During challenging intervals, regularity in any realm can evaporate—and the loss of predictability is disorienting. Maintaining a semblance of the familiar brings comfort during moments of chaos. Amid disruption, I can preserve regularity as much as possible or create new routines to accommodate a change in my circumstances or bandwidth.

As I navigate life and motherhood, the anchors of rhythm are reassuring to me as well as to my child.

tonight,
*I discover
meditative
moments.*

I look to the recurring tasks of daily life, the physical things I do regularly as a matter of course.

* * *

The repetitive, physical routines of washing dishes, taking a shower, tidying up, doing laundry, or brushing my teeth are convenient meditation points. Familiar and straightforward, these actions are opportunities for embodiment and presence. When I'm washing the dishes, I can let go of thoughts and focus on my senses. I can absorb the experience of dishwashing: the temperature and sensation of water, the smell of soap, the texture of objects, how my body feels standing in the kitchen.

I can bring a sensory practice into everyday moments and reveal the pleasantness of many regular activities.

tonight,

I am sad.

I acknowledge
my melancholy.

* * *

Unhappiness is more intense when I'm tired, when the fatigue feels raw and shapeless. Sometimes sadness comes from nowhere at all, and sentiment spills as it will. I allow the blue wave to wash over me, trusting that sorrow often ebbs in daylight, and that even a little bit of sleep will lessen the burden and the bittersweet. And when it doesn't, when it's too much to bear, I can reach for guidance and support. I don't need to endure on my own.

*I can ask for help when
sadness feels impossible, just as
I would want my child to do.*

tonight,
*I reflect
on my family's
creed.*

I think about the identity of my family and how we function as a whole.

* * *

The essence of a group, large or small, is the cohesion that grows from shared values, priorities, and purpose. Engaging my family in creating a common creed, a family mission statement, helps each of us know who we are and where we're going, individually and together. What defines us as a family? How do we want each family member to feel within our home? What do we care about as a group?

Our family creed can establish how we treat each other, support each other, and make a difference in the world we share.

I envision my
home as a nest.

✳ ✳ ✳

In the context of raising my child, I consider the purposes I want my home to serve. What emotional materials are most essential for its construction? Which elements make our home safe, secure, comfortable, and nurturing? With what softness do I line its interior? I build and foster this nest with a watchful mama's eye, making repairs over the years and adding twigs as needed.

One day this nest will be empty,
its purpose in fledgling launch served,
and I will know I built it well.

tonight,

I honor my child's own compass.

132

I contemplate the goals and direction my child may one day have.

✳ ✳ ✳

I don't know what the future will bring as it reveals my child's aptitudes, interests, and dreams, but I do know that exploration and discovery lie ahead. In considering my role as supporter, encourager, and adviser, I acknowledge that my child's goals may be different—perhaps quite different—from my goals for my child.

To help my child grow into a self-actualized and satisfying adulthood, I can encourage who and what my child wants to be.

tonight,
*I celebrate
creativity.*

134

I recognize the many ways in which I am creative.

* * *

Conception, pregnancy, and childbirth are profoundly creative processes, but they don't compare to the consciously creative work of motherhood. As a mother, I continually make something from nothing, make do, make it up, and make it work. In addition to developing adaptive flexibility, engaging in personal creative work—in the realm of creative arts or anything generative that appeals to me—is a means to understanding the astounding journey of personhood.

*Exercising creativity—
whether through personal projects
or as part of the motherhood journey—
helps me see value in the process
rather than its outcome.*

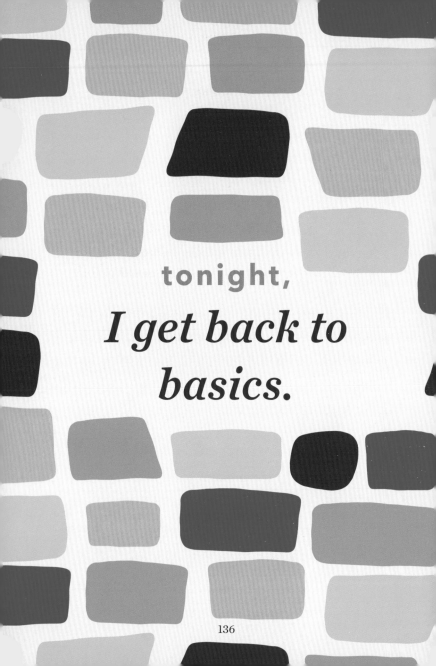

tonight,

I get back to basics.

I decipher the bare minimum of my "have-to" list.

* * *

When my life circumstances are unusually demanding, I can adjust expectations. I can be clear with myself and with others about what I'm going to do and what I'm not going to do. The true daily necessities are keeping my family sheltered, fed, and clothed. Anything unrelated to meeting these basic needs is optional. When I can't do any more, I can do less.

—————————————————

Defining my bare minimum enables me to navigate overwhelming circumstances with less stress, less guilt, and more clarity.

—————————————————

tonight,
I fast-
forward.

I imagine what my child will be like at my age.

* * *

It stretches my imagination to think of my child as an adult with all the responsibilities, milestones, challenges, and celebrations of adulthood. The future is an infinite array of possibilities. What will my child be like as an independent adult? Decades from now, I will observe my grown child in wonder, marveling at all that has transpired. As my child grows and matures, so too will our relationship grow and mature. We have so much to experience.

One day my child and I will interact as two adults— while at the same time, forever mother and child.

tonight,
*I stop
making worry
an event.*

I resolve not to let circumstances look bigger than they are.

* * *

Special occasions are not exempt from late-night interludes of mothering. The eve of a major holiday, birthday, vacation, work event, family celebration— sometimes the night before an important day coincides with inadequate sleep. Awake on these nights, I'm aware of all that will need doing tomorrow. Rather than worry, I can focus on what I am able to control and ask for help when the time comes.

_I let go of what doesn't matter
in the bigger picture, and stay open
to the arrival of help, resources,
and gifts I cannot foresee._

tonight,

I wonder at seasons.

I celebrate the ebb and flow of seasons of the year and seasons of life.

* * *

Sometimes a circumstance or chapter feels over, lost, or complete—but in truth it is only dormant and will bloom again in time. As fallow fields regenerate, nutrients gather in layers below the surface. This unseen potential for new life is a gift. The cycle of each season is a revel of experience.

I welcome each season's invitation to engage my senses and live fully in what arises, embracing the gift of seasonal renewal.

tonight,
I respect learning on the job.

I acknowledge that motherhood is not a plug-and-play enterprise.

* * *

No amount of observation, research, or planning is adequate preparation for this role; the only way to learn it is to do it. I brought to this job my firsthand experience of childhood, observations of the mothers around me, cultural norms, and my personal physiological traits. I am completely unique in motherhood, as all mothers are, and no more or less equipped.

I can trust in my mothering signature. Day by day, year by year, I acquire all of the capabilities and knowledge I need.

tonight,
I capture my midnight thoughts.

I appreciate those curious ideas that emerge in late hours.

* * *

When fatigue loosens my brain, sometimes interesting ideas spark in non sequitur fireworks. Many of these thoughts feel important or useful or have creative potential. While my memory might not preserve these ideas, I can keep index cards and a writing implement at hand in the places where I sit and sleep. When I capture this array of random thoughts and big ideas, one per card, over time these snippets will accumulate into a stack of possibilities and snapshots of moments otherwise forgotten.

The thoughts and observations that emerge during my wakeful nighttime hours are ripe for creative harvest.

tonight, *I welcome laughter.*

I remember that laughter is medicine for body and spirit.

Sometimes laughter is the best response to the absurdity of life. In addition to diffusing tension, laughter is relaxing and increases resilience. It's beneficial to my heart, immune system, and life span. Laughing strengthens relationships and triggers endorphins. And it feels so good, it's contagious. What is more irresistible than the laughter of a baby, or more delightful than the silver-bell laughter of a child? We laugh together.

With shared amusement
and a lightness of being,
I remind myself to succumb to
hilarity when it presents itself,
and sometimes, even
when it doesn't.

tonight,
*I give myself
a break.*

I plan an hour in which I am responsible for only myself.

* * *

I promise myself sixty minutes of solitude that serve my personal benefit and restoration. I ponder the possibilities. What do I want to do with that time? What do I really need right now? How might I fulfill a part of those needs with an hour to myself? I envision my ideal hour unfolding: where I am, what I'm doing, how I feel.

*Arranging a short
self-care session is
an investment in myself
that only I can make.*

tonight,
I am myself.

I remind myself that motherhood is not a competitive sport.

* * *

In life and in the digital world, I encounter mothers who seem to be doing amazing things and raising amazing children while looking amazing and living amazing lives. It appears effortless. I know that this exterior glimpse is at best only a highlight reel, and at worst, a façade. It's not inspiration if it makes me feel inferior or lacking.

I am more centered, confident, and authentic when I stay focused on the reality of my own life, in all its full-color, 24/7 glory.

tonight,
I honor
movement.

**I remember that
baby steps, tiny as they may be,
are forward progress.**

* * *

Sometimes I can only do a little bit, even though I'd like to do more. This mismatch between bandwidth and purpose can be frustrating. In disappointment, I could decide not to bother with any of it. I might move the task or project into the "someday" category or opt to abandon it entirely. But taking one small step is far better than taking none at all—because action creates momentum from intention.

*My surest path to progress
is movement,
however modest it may be.*

tonight,
I lower the shield.

I want to protect my child from pain.

* * *

I cannot shield my child from every fall, hurt, disappointment, or loss—and I know it would not benefit my child to do so. Instead, I can equip my child with the self-confidence and resiliency to handle what life brings. Not many generations ago, children roamed freely, largely unsupervised, figuring out how to interact with each other and the world. In doing so, they gained independence and agency.

I can support my child in the positive risk-taking and exploration that build a sense of self.

tonight,
*I appreciate
my journey.*

I realize how motherhood has changed the way I look at life.

* * *

I can see more broadly, as if my peripheral vision has expanded—and at the same time, the things that really matter to me have condensed and focused. Sometimes it's difficult to remember what my life used to be like, what I did with my time, and how and why I made the decisions I made. I know more now—and I'm also more aware of all I have yet to learn.

This extraordinary journey continues to change me and expand my experience in ways that will forever be part of who I am.